March of America Facsimile Series

Number 24

The Discovery of New Brittaine

Edward Bland

The Discovery of
New Brittaine

by Edward Bland

ANN ARBOR

UNIVERSITY MICROFILMS, INC.

A Subsidiary of Xerox Corporation

Foreword

The Discovery of New Brittaine, written by Edward Bland
and published in London in 1651, relates the explorations
achieved by the author and a few companions from Virginia
into what is now the border region of North Carolina and Virginia. Bland's account illustrates how colonial expansion was
carried forward from established bases in Virginia and the
manner in which explorers sometimes attempted to profit from
their discoveries.

Edward Bland had been sent by his brother, a member of
the Old Virginia Company, to help manage lands in that col-
ony. While in Virginia, Bland and several companions explored
the region below the James River which they named New
Britain. Convinced that he had found a country ideal for settlement, Bland petitioned the Virginia Assembly on his return
for authority to settle it. He then sailed back to England to
recruit colonists. The Virginia Assembly granted Bland's peti-
tion on condition that he find "a hundred able men sufficiently
furnished with Armes and Munition." It was to attract settlers
and to fulfill this condition that Bland wrote and published
what was essentially his travel journal.

Bland appealed first to the higher ideals of his readers. "Who
ever thou art that desirest the Advancement of Gods glory by
conversion of the Indians, [and] the Augmentation of the English Common-wealth, in extending its liberties" would be well
advised, he wrote, to settle in New Britain. However Bland
marshaled many other reasons for settlement there. He noted
in a rather obvious fashion that New Britain was located in the

same latitude in which Sir Walter Raleigh had placed the Garden of Eden. He observed that the country enjoyed a more temperate climate than that of England. He suggested that settlement in New Britain would avoid "all inconveniencies... which commonly attend New Plantations, being supplied with necessaries from the Neighbourhood of Virginia." Salt and fish were in good supply, he said, and it would be possible to raise tobacco and possibly sugar cane. He waxed enthusiastic about the "very much exceeding rich, red, fat, marle Land." As an added touch he remarked that "'tis very probable that there may be Gold, and other Mettals amongst the hils."

In spite of all his superlatives, Bland's colonization project did not materialize. Bland's death about 1653 concluded the episode. A map showing the general area of Virginia and New Britain accompanies the text. For more information about Bland and his explorations see the introduction by Howard H. Peckham to Edward Bland, *The Discovery of New Britain* ([Ann Arbor], 1954), and also Clarence W. Alvord and Lee Bidgood, *The First Explorations of the Trans-Allegheny Region by the Virginians, 1650-1674* (Cleveland, 1912), pp. 47-51.

The Discovery of New Brittaine

THE
DISCOVERY
OF
Nevv Brittaine.

Began *August* 27. *Anno Dom.* 1650.

By {
Edward Bland, Merchant.
Abraham Woode, Captaine.
Sackford Brewster, } Gentlemen.
Elias Pennant,
}

From Fort *Henry*, at the head of *Appamattuck* River in *Virginia*, to the Fals of *Blandina*, firſt River in *New Brittaine*, which runneth Weſt; being 120. Mile South-weſt, between 35. & 37. degrees, (a pleaſant Country,) of temperate Ayre, and fertile Soyle.

LONDON,
Printed by *Thomas Harper* for *John Stephenson*, at the
Sun below Ludgate. *M.DC.LI.*

To the Reader.

Ho ever thou art that defireſt the Advancement of Gods glory by converſion of the Indians, the Augmentation of the Engliſh Commonwealth, in extending its liberties; I would adviſe thee to conſider the preſent benefit and future profits that will ariſe in the wel ſetling Virginia's Confines, eſpecially that happy Country of New Brittaine, in the Latitude of 35. and 37. degrees, of more temperate Clymate then that the Engliſh now inhabite, abounding with great Rivers of long extent, and encompaſſing a great part, or moſt of Virginia's Continent; a place ſo eaſie to be ſettled in, in regard that Horſe and Cattle in foure or five dayes may be conveyed for the benefit of Undertakers, and all inconveniencies avoyded which com-

monly

commonly attend *New Plantations*, being *supplied with ne-cessaries from the Neighbourhood of* Virginia.

That the *Assembly of* Virginia *(as may be seene by their Order since my returne heereto procured) have conceived a hundred to be a sufficient force and competence for the establishment of that Country in which Tobacco will grow larger and more in quantity. Sugar Canes are supposed naturally to be there, or at least if implanted will undoubtedly flourish: For we brought with us thence extraordinary Canes of twenty five foot long and six inches round; there is also great store of fish, and the Inhabitants relate that there is plenty of Salt made to the Sunne without art; Tobacco Pipes have beene seene among these Indians tipt with Silver, and they weare Copper Plates about their necks: They have two Crops of Indian Corne yearely, whereas* Virginia *hath but one. what I write, is what I have proved; I cordially wish some more then private Spirits would take it into their consideration; so may it prove most advantagious to particular and publick ends; for which so prayeth,*

Your faithfull fervant,

Edward Bland.

October

October 20. 1650. By the Assembly

 *T is Ordered by the Grand Assembly, that according to the Petition of Mr. Edward Bland, Merchant, that he the sayd Bland, or any other be permitted to discover and seate to the Southward in any convenient place where they discover; and that according to his Petition for furthering his Designes hee bee permitted to have correspondence with the Indians, and also receive the benevolence of the well-affected, and use all lawfull meanes for effecting thereof, provided that they secure themselves in effecting the sayd Designe with a hundred able men sufficiently furnished with Armes and Munition.*

John Corkes, Cler., Dom. Com.

The

8   **3 9**   **4 0**   **4 1**

Scala Miliarum

10. 20. 30. 40. 50. 60. 70. 80. 90. 100

A mapp of Virginia discouered to y^e Hills, and in it's Latt: From 35. deg: & ½ neer Florida, to 41. deg: bounds of new England

Noua

Francia

...ad of Iames Riuer, ouer these hills ...necessarily must run into ye peacefull ...all true English.

A Mighty great ...

Massomonckei Cr.

Canada flu:

I A, & a new

MARY LAND

Eldery

Sweeds Holla-d

the Lord Baltimors Plantation begun 1635.

Plant... Plant...

Axion

Noua Albion

Eriwom

Annedale C

Wilkiss riuer.

Checepiacke 200 miles long

Sasquesahanoug Riuer...

...this is and call their Albion

Mont Ployden

Raritás

Elk riuer

Tehenok riuer

This Riuer the Lord Ployden hath a Patten of and haue a great of Furrs.

Cape Iames

Lord Delawars Bay and Riuer

but the Sweeds are planted in it, and haue a plantation and

Hanteok

This Riuer the Dutch haue a plantation and

A great trade of Furrs

Richnek woods

Cape May

C V M Eggbay

Conetteqnt Ri:

Hudsons

Long Island Cape Codd

Ludgate. 1651

Sir *Walter Rawleighs* Obſervation on 35. degrees Latitude.

PAradiſe was created a part of this Earth, and ſeated in the lower part of Eden *or* Meſopotamia *, containing alſo a part of* Shinar *and* Armenia *; it ſtands 35 degrees from the* Equinoctiall *, and 55 from the North-pole , in a temperate Climate, full of excellent fruits, chiefely of Palme-trees without labour ; for whereinſoever the* Earth, Nature, *and the* Sun *can moſt vaunt that they have excelled, yet ſhall the* Palme-tree *be the greateſt wonder of all their workes : This tree alone giveth unto man whatſoever his life beggeth at* Natures hand. *The like are alſo found both in the* Eaſt *and* weſt-Indies *as well as in* Paradiſe *, which Countries are alſo bleſſed with a perpetuall* Spring *and* Summer *, &c.* Rawleighs Marrow of Hiſtory, Page 42.*

By how much Adam *exceeded all living men in perfection , by being the immediate workmanſhip of* God *, by ſo much did that choſen, and particular Garden exceed all the parts of the* Univerſall *world in which* God *had planted the* Trees *of* Life, *and* Knowledge, *Plants onely proper, and belonging to the* Paradiſe, *and Garden, of ſo great a* Lord. Ibid. p. 43.*

The

The Discovery of New Britaine.

Uguſt 27. 1650. *The Right Honorable Sir* W.Berkly, *Kt. being Governour and Captaine Generall of* Virginia, Edw. Bland *Merch.* Abraham Wood *Capt.* ·Elias Ponnant *and* Sackford Brewſter *Gent.* *foure Men, and one Indian named* Pyancha, *an Appamattuck for our Guide, with two ſervants, foure Horſes and Proviſion, advanced from* Fort Henry, *lying on Appamattuck River at the fals, being a branch of* James River, *intending a South weſterne Diſcovery.*

This day wee paſſed over a branch belonging to *Blackwater* lake, running South eaſt into *Chawan* River; at that place wee were forced to unlade our Carriages by reaſon of the great raines lately fallen, which otherwiſe is very paſſable for foot,being firm gravelly ground in the bottome, and lieth from Fort *Henry* 20. miles,and ſome 12.miles from this place we travelled unto a deepe River called the *Nottaway* Creeke ſome 100.paces over ſandy bottomes(& with a little labour may be made paſſeable) unto a *Nottaway* Town liyng ſome two miles from the River. Hither we came within night, and by reaſon of our ſuddaine approach and hallowing of *Robert Farmer* ſervant to Mr. *Bland,* the Inhabitants ran all away into the Woods, with their Women and Children ; therefore by us it was named *Farmers* Chaſe. After our arrivall there within a ſmall ſpace of time one *Indian* man appeared,and finding of us peaceable, and the white flag bore before us by our Guide whom they knew, he made a

B   hallow,

hallow and the reft came in from their fculking holes
like fo many timerous Hares, and fhewed us what
curtefic they could. About two houres after came to
us *Oyeocker* elder brother to *Chounterounte* one of the
Nottaway Kings, who told us that his brother *Chounte-*
rounte, and other of the *Nottaway* Kings would come
to us next day by Noone, and that the day before
Chounterounte and all his men had been a hunting,and
it hapned that *Chounterounte* had fhot one of his bro-
thers in the leg, and that thereupon he was gone
downewards. We ftayed untill next day at Noone
but he came not, and then we journyed unto the
Towne belonging unto *Oyeocker*, who kindly invited
us thither, and told us he thought that *Chounterounte*
would meet us there, and alfo of his owne accord
proffered us to be our guide whitherfoever we went.
The Land generally to this Towne is Champion, very rich, and the Towne fcituate in a rich levell, well
timbered, watered,and very convenient for Hogs and
Cattle.

Auguft 28. We journied with our new entertain-
ed Guide *Oyeocker*, lying betweene South, and South
and by Weft, from the firft Towne upon a very rich
levell of Land: fixteen miles from this place we came
unto the River *Penna* Mount, being another branch of
Chawan River,eight miles on the South fide it hath very rich Land and Corn-fields on both fides the River,
and is about fome 200. paces wide, and runs out with
elbowes: at the place of our paffage over this River to
this fecond Towne is fhallow upon a Sandy Point,and
with a very little labour may be made paffeable
both for foot and horfe, or any Carriage by Land,

or

or pentater with small Boats, and some two miles higher there is a found passage no deeper then a mans anckle : Within night came *Chounterounte* unto our Quarters frowning, and with a countenance noting much discontent, downe he sets, and lookes about him, salutes the English with a scornefull posture, and then our Appamattack Guide, and tels him, I am sorry for thee friend, thou wilt be knockt on the head ; after this some pause was made before any discourse, expecting the English would begin, but finding us flow, he thus spake : There was a *Wainoake Indian* told him that there was an Englishman a *Cockarous* hard by Captaine *Floods*, gave this Indian Bells, and other petty truck to lay downe to the *Tuskarood* King, and would have hired him to have gone with him, but the *wainoakes* being doubtfull what to doe, went to Captaine *Flood* for advice, who advised them not to go, for that the Governour would give no licence to go thither ; heereupon *Chounterounte* was by us questioned, when and who it was that had told him so, & if he did know that *wainoake* Indian, to which he answered doubtfully, and demanded of us whither we did intend to go ; we told him the *Tuskarood* King had envited us to trade, and our Governour had ordered us to go, and speake with an Englishman amongst them, and to enquire for an English woman cast away long since, and was amongst those Nations. *Chounterounte* perswaded us to go no further, alleadging there was no English there, that the way was long, for passage very bad by reason of much raine that had lately fallen, and many rotten Marrishes and Swampps there was to passe over, *in fine we*

A 2   found

found him, and all his men very unwilling we fhould go any further; but we told them,that let the waies and paffages be never fo bad, we were refolved to go through, and that we were not afraid of him nor his Nation, nor any other, for we intended no injury,and that we muft go, for we were commanded by our King; thefe words caufed *Chounterounte* to affimulate a feare in his countenance,and after delivery of him-felfe,at our going away next day,when we had moun-ted our Horfes, *Chounterounte* came privately unto us, and in a moft ferious manner intimating unto us,that he loved us, and our Nation, and that he lively ap-prehended our danger, and that our fafety concerned him, for if any accident hapned otherwife then good to us, he fhould be fufpected to have a hand in it, and withall wifhed us to go no further, for that he cer-tainly knew that the Nations we were to go through would make us away by treachery;we anfwered him, that we were not afraid to be killed, for that any one of us were able to deale with forty through the pro-tection of our great God,for we were commanded by our King.

Auguft 29. We travelled from this fecond Town to *Maharineck*, eight miles upon barren Champion Lands, and fix miles further is a branch that runnes South weft,with rich Lands upon it; and from thence fome fixe miles further, is a Brooke fome hundred paces over, and runnes South and a little to the Weft, on both fides of the Creek : for fowre miles or there-abouts,is very rich Lands,well Timbered and Wate-red, and large dry Meadowes, South and by Weft : From this Creeke is another, fome eight miles off, that

that opens it felfe into divers fmall Guts, made by
the inundation of Frefhes of Waters ; and the paffage lies fome two hundred paces from the Path,
and this Creek is fome ten miles from *Maharinecke*
Towne, and was by us named *Newcombs Forreft*. It
was night when we entred into *Maharineck*, where
we found a Houfe ready made for us of Matts ; and
Corne ftalkes layd in feverall places for our Horfes,
the Inhabitants ftanding, according to their cuftome,
to greet us : and after fome difcourfe with their *werrowance*, a Youth, to whom wee prefented feverall
gifts, we certified them the caufe of our comming
was to Trade in way of friendfhip, and defired the
great men that what Wares or Skins the Town did
afford, might be brought to our Quarters next morning ; and alfo a meafure for *Roanoak*, which they
promifed fhould be done, and fo left us to our felves
a while, untill wee had refrefhed our felves with fuch
provifions as they had fet before us, in moft plenti-
full maner ; and afterwards the great men and Inhabitants came, and performed divers Ceremonies, anc
Dancings before us, as they ufe to doe to their grea
Emperour *Apachancano*, when they entertain him in
moft folemne maner and friendfhip.

Auguft 30. Being wearied with our laft dayes travell, we continued at *Maharineck*, and this day fpake
with a Tuskarood Indian, who told us that the Eng-
lifhman was a great way off at the furtherTuskarood
Towne, and wee hired this Turkarood Indian to run
before, and tell his *werrowance* wee intended to lay
him downe a prefent at *Hocomowanonek*, and defired
to have him meete us there, and alfo wrote to that

effect

effect to the Englishman in English, Latine, Span sh, French and Dutch, the *Tuskarood* promised in three dayes to meete us at *Hocomawananck*. In the afternoone came two Indians to our Quarters, one of whom the *Maharinecks* told us was the *werrowance* of *Hocomawananck* River, seemed very joyfull that wee could goe thither, and told us the *Tuskarood* would have come to us to trade, but that the *wainoakes* had spoken much to dishearten them from having any trade with the English, and that they intended divers times to have come in, but were afraid, for the *wainoakes* had told them that the English would kill them, or detaine them, and would not let them goe without a great heape of *Roanoake* middle high, to which we answered that the *wainoakes* durst not affirme any such thing to our faces, and that they had likewise spoken much against the *Tuskarood* to the English, it being a common thing amongst them to villefie one another, and tell nothing but lies to the English.

This day in the morning the *Maharineck* great men spake to heare some of our guns go off: Whereupon we shot two guns at a small marke, both hitting it, and at so great a distance of a hundred paces, or more, that the Indians admired at it: And a little before night the old King of *Maharineck* came to us, and told us, that the people in the Towne were afraid when the guns went off, and ran all away into the Woods. This night also we had much Dancing.

August 31. Wee went away from *Maharineck* South East two miles to goe over *Maharineck* River, which hath a bottome betweene two high land sides
through

through which you muſt paſſe to get over, which River is about two hundred paces broad, and hath a high water marke after a freſh of at leaſt twenty foot perpendicular by the trees in the breaches betweene the River, and the high land of the old fields. This River is the Southerly laſt and maine branch of *Chawan* River, and was by us named *woodford* River, and runs to the Eaſtward of the South. On both ſides of *woodford* River is very much exceeding rich Land, but eſpecially on the further ſide towards *Hocomawananck*. Imediately after the paſſage over this River, are old Indian fields of exceeding rich Land, that beare two Crops of Indian Corne a yeare, and hath timber trees above five foot over, whoſe truncks are a hundred foot in cleare timber, which will make twenty Cuts of Board timber a piece, and of theſe there is abundance.

As alſo exceeding rich Land, full of great Reeds thrice as big as the largeſt Arrow Reeds we have about our Plantations; this good Land continues for ſome ſix miles together unto a great Swampp, and then begins a pyny barren Champion Land with divers Branches and Pecoſans, yet very paſſeable, running South and by Weſt, unto a deepe River ſome a hundred paces over, running South, and a little to the Eaſt, which River incloſes a ſmall Iſland which wee named *Brewſters* Iſland, ſome eighteene miles from *woodford* River due South, and by Weſt, with very exceeding rich Land on both ſides of it for ſome ſixe miles together, and this River we alſo named *Brewſters* River, it being the firſt branch of *Hocomawananck* River: and a little lower downe as the River runs, is
ſuch

such another River as *Chickahamine* River (which is a mile broad.)

After we had paffed over this River we travelled fome twenty miles, further upon a pyny barren Champicn Land to *Hocomawananck* River, South, and by Weft: fome twelve miles from *Brewfters* River we came unto a path running croffe fome twenty yards on each fide unto two remarkeable Trees ; at this path our Appamattuck Guide made a ftop, and cleared the Wefterly end of the path with his foote, being demanded the meaning of it, he fhewed an unwillingneffe to relate it, fighing very much : Whereupon we made a ftop untill *Oyeocker* our other Guide came up, and then our Appamattuck Guide journied on ; but *Oyeocker* at his comming up cleared the other end of the path, and prepared himfelfe in a moft ferious manner to require our attentions, and told us that many yeares fince their late great Emperour *Appachancano* came thither to make a War upon the *Tuskarood*, in revenge of three of his men killed, and one wounded, who efcaped, and brought him word of the other three murthered by the *Hocomawananck* Indians for lucre of the *Roanoake* they brought with them to trade for Otter skins. There accompanyed *Appachancano* feverall petty Kings that were under him, amongft which there was one King of a Towne called *Pawhatan*, which had long time harboured a grudge againft the King of *Chawan*, about a yong woman that the King of *Chawan* had detayned of the King of *Pawhatan* : Now it hapned that the King of *Chawan* was invited by the King of *Pawhatan* to this place under pretence to prefent him with a Guift of
fome

fome great vallew, and there they met accordingly,
and the King of *Pawhatan* went to falute and embrace
the King of *Chawan*, and ftroaking of him after their
ufuall manner, he whipt a bow ftring about the
King of *Chawans* neck, and ftrangled him; and how
that in memoriall of this, the path is continued unto
this day, and the friends of the *Pawhatans* when they
paffe that way, cleanfe the Wefterly end of the path,
and the friends of the *Chawans* the other. And fome
two miles from this path we came unto an Indian
Grave upon the Eaft fide of the path : Upon which
Grave there lay a great heape of fticks covered with
greene boughs, we demanded the reafon of it, *Oyeoc-*
ker told us, that there lay a great man of the *Chawans*
that dyed in the fame quarrell, and in honour of his
memory they continue greene boughs over his Grave
to this day, and ever when they goe forth to Warre
they relate his, and others valorous, loyall Acts, to
their yong men, to annimate them to doe the like
when occafion requires. Some foure miles from *Ho-*
comawananck is very rich Champian Land: It was
night when we came to *Hocomawananck* River, and the
Indian that came with us from *Woodford* River, and
belonged to *Hocomawananck*, would have had us quartered upon the fide of a great Swampp that had the
advantage of feverall bottomes of the Swampp on
both fides of us, but we removed to take our advantage for fafety, and retreate, in cafe any accident
fhould happen, which at that time promifed nothing
but danger, for our Guides began to be doubtfull, and
told us, that the *Hocomawananck* Indians were very
treacherous, and that they did not like their counte-
B   nances,

nances, and shape well; this place we named *Py-anchas* Parke: about three houres after we had taken up our Quarters, some of the Inhabitants came, and brought us roasting eares, and Sturgeon, and the *Ho-comawananck* Indian that came with us from *Woodford* River, came not unto us untill next day, but his *War-rowance* told us before wee came from *Woodford*, hee could not come untill that day at night. The next day morning after our comming to *Hocomawananck* the In-habitants seemed to prepare us a house: But we a-bout eight of the clock set forward to goe view the place where they killed Sturgeon, which was some six miles from the place where we quartered by *Pyan-chas* Parke, where there is a River Running very deep South, exceeding deepe, and foure hundred paces broad. The high water marke of this River between both sides of the River perpendicular, from the top of the Banck to the River, is forty five foot upon a fresh; this River was by us named *Blandina* River: from *Py-anchas* Parke to the place where they kill Sturgeon is six miles up the River running Northerly, and all ex-ceeding rich Land: Both upwards and downewards upon the River, at this place where they kill Sturge-on also are the Falls, and at the foot of these Falls al-so lies two Islands in a great Bay, the uppermost whereof Mr. *Blande* named *Charles* Island, and the lowermost Captaine *Wood* named *Berkeley* Island: on the further side of these Islands the Bay runs naviga-ble by the two Islands sides: *Charles* Island is three miles broad, and foure miles long, and *Berkeley* Island almost as big, both in a manner impregnable, by na-ture being fortified with high Clefts of Rocky Stone,

and

and hardly paſſeable , without a way cut through
them , and conſiſts all of exceeding rich Land , and
cleare fields , wherein growes Canes of a foot about,
and of one yeares growth Canes that a reaſonable
hand can hardly ſpan ; and the Indians told us they
were very ſweet, and that at ſome time of the yeare
they did ſuck them, and eate them, and of thoſe we
brought ſome away with us. The Land over againſt
Charles Iſland we named *Blands* Diſcovery , and the
Land over againſt *Berkeley* Iſland we named *woods*
journy , and at the lower end of *Charles* Iſland lies a
Bay due South from the ſaid Iſland , ſo ſpatious that
we could not ſee the other ſide of it:this bay we named *Pennants* Bay , and in the River between *Charles* I-
ſland, and the maine Land lies a Rocky Point in the
River, which Point comes out of *Charles* Iſland , and
runs into the middle of the River:this Point we named *Brewſters* Point, and at this Point only , and no o-
ther is there any place paſſeable into *Charles* Iſland,
and this *Brewſters* Point runs not quite from *Charles*
Iſland to the maine Land,but when you come off the
maine Land to the Rivers ſide, you muſt wade about
fifty paces to come upon the Point , and if you miſſe
the Point on either ſide, up or downe the River, you
muſt ſwim,and the River runs very ſwift. Some three
miles from the River ſide over againſt *Charles* Iſland
is a place of ſeverall great heapes of bones,and heere
the Indian belonging to *Blandina* River that went a-
long with us to the Fals, ſat downe,and ſeemed to be
much diſcontented , inſomuch that he ſhed teares ;
we demanded why thoſe bones were piled up ſo cu-
riouſly ? *Oyeocker* told us, that at this place *Appachan-*

came one morning with 400. men treacherously flew
240. of the *Blandina* River Indians in revenge of three
great men slaine by them , and the place we named
Golgotha ; as we were going to *Blandina* River we
spake to *Oyeocker* our Guide to lead us the way, and
he would not ; but asked our Appamattuck Guide
why we did not get us gone, for the Inhabitants were
jealous of us, and angry with us, and that the Runner
we sent to the *Tuskarood* would not come at the day
appointed, nor his King, but ran another way , and
told the Indians that we came to cut them off; whereupon our Appamattuck Guide stepped forth , and
frowning said , come along, we will go see the Falls,
and so led the way, and also told us that the *woodford*
Indians lied, and that Indian that came to us, which
the *woodford* Indian said was the King of *Blandina* River, was not the *werrowance* of *Blandina* River; whereupon we resolved to return (having named the whole
Continent *New Brittaine*) another way into our. old
path that led to *Brewsters* River, and shot off no guns
because of making a commotion , and adding to the
Natives feares. At *Blandina* River we had some dif-
course with our Appamattuck Guide concerning that
River, who told us that that Branch of *Blandina* River
ran a great way up into the Country ; and that about
three dayes journy further to the South-West, there
was a far greater Branch so broad that a man could
hardly see over it , and bended it selfe to the North-
ward above the head of *James* River, unto the foot
of the great Mountaines, on which River there lived
many people upwards, being the *Occonacheans* and the
Nessoneicks , and that where some of the *Occonacheans*
lived,

lived, there is an Iſland within the River three dayes journy about, which is of a very rich and fertile ſoile, and that the upper end of the Iſland is fordable, not above knee deepe, of a ſtony bottome, running very ſwift, and the other ſide very deepe and navigable: Alſo we found many of the people of *Blandina* River to have beards, and both there, and at *Woodford* River we ſaw many very old men, and that the Climate according to our opinions was far more temperate then ours of *Virginia,* and the Inhabitants full of Children; they alſo told us that at the bottome of the River was great heapes of Salt; and we ſaw among them Copper, and were informed that they tip their pipes with ſilver, of which ſome have been brought into this Country, and 'tis very probable that there may be Gold, and other Mettals amongſt the hils.

September 1. About noone from Woods Journey wee travelled ſome ſixe miles North Eaſt, unto the old Path that leads to *Brewſters* River : within night we quartered on the other ſide of it, and kept good watch : this Path runnes from Woods Journey north and by Eaſt, and due North.

September 2. In the morning about eight of the clocke, as every one was mounted, came to our quarters *Occonnoſquay*, ſonne to the Tuskarood King, and another Indian whom he told was a *werrowance,* and his Kinſeman, with the Runner which wee had ſent to the Tuskarood King, who was to meet us at *Blandina* River that night; the Kings ſonne told us that the Engliſh man would be at his houſe that night; a great way off ; and would have had us gone backe with him, but we would not, and appointed him to meete

us

us at *woodford* River where hee came not, wee
having some suspition that hee came from *woodford* River that night, and that our Runner had
not beene where we had sent him, through some
information of our Nottaway guide, which afterwards proved true, by the Relation of the *werrowance*
of *Blandina* River, whom about fowre howres after
wee had parted with the Kings son, wee met on the
way comming from *woodford* River with a company
of men, thinking he should have found us at *Blandina*
River that night, according to his order and promise;
with whom falling into discourse, he told us that the
King of the *Tuskaroods* son, and our Runner were the
night before at *woodford* River; but the Kings son told
us he came from *Blandina* River, and beyond, and
hearing we were gone before he came, he had travelled all night from *Blandina* River to overtake us.
This day about Noone we came to *woodford* River
Towne, and tarried there that night, we found the
old *werrowance*, and all his great men gone, yet had
courteous quarter; but not without great grounds of
suspition, and signes that they were angry at us: at
our coming back to *woodford* River we had information that some Spies of *wainoake* had been there a little before we came, and that the King of *wainoake* and
Chounterounte had sent Runners to all the Nations
thereabouts, informing them that the English were
come to cut them off, which we supposed to be some
greater Polititians then Indian Consultations, who
had some private ends to themselves, and minded nothing lesse then a publick good; for we found that the
Runner whom we imployed to carry our message to
                                                    the

the *Tuskarood* King, ran to the *Waynoakes*, and he whom
the *Woodford* Indians told us was the *Werrowance* of
Blandina River, was a *Woodford* Indian, and no *Werrowance*, but done of purpose to get something out of us,
and we had information that at that time there were
other English amongst the Indians.

September 3. By breake of day we journied from
Woodford River to a path some eight miles above *Pennants* Mount running North, and by East and North,
North, East, which was done by the advice of our
Appamattuck Guide, who told us that he was informed that some plots might be acted against us, if we
returned the way that we came, for we told *Chounterounte* we would returne the same way againe: And
this information our Guide told us he had from a woman that was his Sweet-heart belonging to *Woodford*
River. This day we passed over very much rich, red,
fat, marle Land, betweene *Woodford* River Towne,
and the head of *Pennants* Mount, with divers Indian
fields; the head of which River abounds much with
great Rocks of Stone, and is two hundred paces over,
and hath a small Island in it named *Sackfords* Island.
Betweene *Pennants* Mount River head, and the head
of *Farmers* Chase River is very much exceeding rich,
red, fat, marle Land, and *Nottaway* and *Schockoores* old
fields, for a matter of sixe miles together all the trees
are blowne up or dead: Heere it began to raine, and
some six miles further we tooke up our quarters, and
it proved a very wet night. At the first other *Nottaway* old fields, we found the Inhabitants much per-
plexed about a gun that went off to the Westward
of them, the night before wee came thither, which
our

our Appamattuck Guide conceived were the Wainoake Spies, set out there to prevent our journyings, and we found severall Agers about the place where the Indians told us the gun went off.

Septemb. 4. About 8 of the Clock we travelled North, North-East some six miles, unto the head of Farmers Chase River, where we were forced to swimm our horses over, by reason of the great rain that fell that night, which otherwise with a little labour may be made very paffable. At this place is very great Rocky stones, fit to make Mill-stones, with very rich tracks of Land, and in some places between the head of Farmers Chase River and Black water Lake, is ground that gives very probable proofe of an Iron, or some other rich Mine. Some sixteen miles from Farmers Chase, North, and by East, and North, North-East, lies Black water Lake, which hath very much rich land about it, and with little labour will be made very paffable. From Black water Lake we did travell to the old fields of *Manks Nessoneicks*, and from thence some 12 miles N. N. East we came unto Fort Henry about the close of the Evening, all well and in good health, notwithstanding from the time we had spoken with *Chounteroonte* at Pennants Mount, we every night kept a strickt watch, having our Swords girt, and our Guns and Pistols by us, for the Indians every night where we lay, kept a strict guard upon us.

The Discoverers, viz:

Mr. *Edward Blande*, Merchant.
Abraham Wood, Captaine.
Mr. *Elias Pennant.*
Mr. *Sackford Brewster.*
Robert *Farmer*, Servant to Mr. *Blande.*
Henry *Newcombe*, Servant to Captaine *Wood.*
Guides. { *Oyeocker*, a Nottaway Werrowance.
{ *Pyancha*, an Appamattuck War Captaine.

F I N I S.

DATE DUE

DEMCO 38-297